I0517790

Whispers of Time

Poems of Family, Faith, and Reflection

Pearl Ashton Talker

Copyright ©2024, Pearl Ashton Talker

ALL RIGHTS RESERVED.

No part of this publication may be reproduced, stored in a retrieval system, or transmitted in any form or by any means—electronic, mechanical, photocopy, recording, or any other—except for brief quotation in reviews, without the prior permission of the author or publisher.

ISBN: 978-1-962402-47-7

The characters, and the incidents in this book are entirely the product of the author's imagination though some events may be based upon fact.

Published by

Fideli Publishing, Inc.
119 W. Morgan St.
Martinsville, IN 46151
www.FideliPublishing.com

Contents

Introduction

The collection of poems in *Whispers of Time* explores various facets of life, love, family, and the human experience. Authored by Pearl Ashton Talker, these verses span themes from personal reflections on aging and loss to the joy of new life and enduring friendships. The poems are deeply introspective, offering a glimpse into the poet's emotional landscape and her philosophical musings on life's journey.

Themes and Motifs

The themes and motifs to be found inside include the following:

Love and Relationships. The recurring theme of love in its various forms—romantic, familial, and platonic—is central to many poems. In "For You" and "Love You So," the poet delves into the depths of romantic love, expressing both its joys and sorrows. The poems often reflect a profound sense of longing and emotional connection.

Family and Generational Bonds. The significance of family is a dominant theme, as seen in poems like "To Albert" and "Your First Grandchild Is Born." These verses celebrate the milestones of family life and the enduring bonds between generations. The poet expresses a deep sense of pride and affection for her family members, highlighting the importance of heritage and continuity.

Reflection and Regret. These include poems such as "Regrets" and "The Children Have Grown" focus on introspection and the passage of time. They explore the feelings of nostalgia and the inevitable changes that come with aging. The poet often reflects on past experiences with a mixture of melancholy and acceptance, acknowledging the bittersweet nature of life.

Nature and Spirituality. Nature serves as a metaphor for life's beauty and transience in many of the poems. "Life's Joyous Gifts" and "A Prayer" evoke the splendor of the natural world and its ability to inspire and heal. Spiritual themes are also present, with poems like "Faith and Prayer" and "Eternal Shadows on the Wall" contemplating the divine and the afterlife.

Resilience and Strength. The theme of resilience is evident in poems such as "Blurry Picture" and "Brave Bird." These works highlight the poet's determination to overcome adversity and find strength in the face of challenges. The imagery of battling against the odds and emerging victorious is a recurring motif, underscoring the human spirit's capacity for endurance.

Stylistic Elements

Pearl Ashton Talker's poetry is characterized by its lyrical quality and emotional depth. The use of vivid imagery and metaphors enriches the reader's experience, bringing the poet's inner world to life. Her verses often employ a rhythmic structure, enhancing the musicality of the poems and making them resonate with readers on an emotional level.

This collection stands as a testament to the enduring power of poetry to articulate the complexities of life and the beauty of the human spirit.

For You

For you, my heart is sighing,
For you, my heart is dying,
For you, my heart is crying,
Just for you.

For you, my love is calling,
For you, my heart is sighing,
For you, I feel I'm dying,
For you, I'm always crying.

Just for you!
You give me happiness,
You give me pain and bliss
With the magic of your kiss.

I long for you.
Oh, how I long for you,
For the love that was so true.
Old love is not as new.

I wait for you.
Come back to hold me tight,
Be with me in the night.
With you, I'll never fight,
Just come back to me!

Love You So

You have made me suffer,
and you've made me cry,
Still, without you, I'd rather die.
I love you so—I don't know why.

With love for you, I always sigh,
I love you, though you're an awful guy.
I love you as much as the sky is high,
You must know it's not a lie.

With you and I, God made a tie.
Who loves you most? It's only I.
Therefore, you must know of my love,
I LOVE YOU, SUNNY BOY!

Absence

When you have left to go so far,
In my sad heart it seems
My life is empty of happiness,
So devoid of dreams.

When evening shadows dance and play,
My heart feels the dark night,
And I search and search in vain
For a starry light.

When you have left and gone so far,
My heart does only know
My steps must quickly follow you
Wherever you go.

Home

A place where our dreams will all come true,
A paradise for me and you,
A living spot of earthly bliss,
A place where we can love and kiss.

A little spot of our very own,
A dear little room we can call our "home,"
God will help us to be happy there,
May our marriage survive all wear and tear.

We'll be setting forth on a new life,
And must avoid all strife,
But work as a team towards one end,
From obstacles our way must wend.

And when many years have weaved their span,
We'll look back where we first began,
And reminisce with tender thought,
As we tell our grandchildren of the joy it brought!

Faith and Prayer

The day I learned my brother had
That dreaded word — "cancer,"
I asked the One above, "Why?" but got no answer.
Pray, pray, have faith in the One above,
The doctor knows what's best for pain — quiet, and love.
Call him, ask him to heal; with our fears he'll help us deal,
For only He knows how we feel.

Waiting in fear outside the operation room,
The doctor came out and relieved our gloom.
The cancerous lump was cut away,
So now we give thanks to Him and pray.

This wonderful man can live on for years,
The prognosis has allayed our fears.

Come and Kiss Me

Come and kiss me, kiss me quick,
Before I throw on you a brick.
Oh, you make me feel so sick,
You damned little country hick.

If only I could give you a kick,
Or put on our love the "mick,"
Or go out with some Dick or Nick—
You know I can take the pick.

So you better be quick,
You stupid, funny little tick,
Before on you I play a trick.

Your First Grandchild is Born

Your first grandchild is born
May many such blessings your life adorn.

Good luck on this happy event
We know how much this has meant.
The hours of expectation spent
On your trip abroad as you went.

May your grandchild grow to be strong and fine
Bringing joy, one can't define.
May God's blessings on her always shine
Baby — Good health, happiness & love be thine.

May you and your wife be blessed
With many grandchildren to attest
Future fruitful years of jest,
Laughter, fun, and all the best.

May your years be filled with bliss.
Every form of happiness.
To your grandchild we give a kiss,
As life's choicest blessings on her we wish.

Ron is Your Name

Ron is your name — Sunshine's Rays
On you, dear baby, shine always,
Now and for all the days.

You're the very precious one,
Your parents hold and say, "Our son".
May your days be full of joy and fun,
May you be your parents' light and sun.

God's blessings shine on you,
Many joys, health and friends true.
Good luck to your family too —
This is what we wish for you.

This Marriage Won't Last Long

We quarreled and we parted time and time again.
The vows made when we started turned out to be in vain.
You left me broken-hearted and caused me grief and pain.

All around us, people said, "This marriage won't last long,"
And when I heard them, my heart bled,
As I prayed we'd prove them wrong.

And so the years have come and gone,
and now we have grown old.
The passions that we felt of yore
Have sweetened to joys untold,
And each day my heart lifts up in prayer and thanks,
For our love that has grown
Through bitterness and wear and tear.

And I raise my head to God in thanks when I see each day.
My heart lifts up in prayer and thanks,
For our love has grown.
Through bitterness and wear and tear,
Into ecstasy which surpasses my dreams of old.

I am glad we stuck it out and did not part forever,
For we would then have never known
The joy we know of now,
The happiness, the perfect bliss,
Of a marriage that could have gone amiss.

Dear Dorit

Dear Dorit, you're a lovely girl,
How you make all hearts whirl.
You really are a gem, a pearl,
Dorit, a pretty doll, but real!

Marry Eran, who does love you,
And to him be really true.
May your love be always new,
Skies be bright and troubles few.

Love, health, and family life,
You'll know its joys when you're a wife.
I only hope you'll know no strife,
Love is possible, but not rife.

Dorit dear, today you're young,
Life's song for you is still unsung.
But I wish for you to be among
Those on whom shine stars and sun.

May life for you be sweet with joy,
Blessed with many a girl and boy.
A long, happy life may you enjoy!

The Children Have Grown

I think as I move in my house each day,
How I'm now lonely and grey.
The children have grown, as it must be,
They no longer have need of me.

I dream of all the years gone by,
Ready to answer their call or cry.
Sons and daughters sat on my knee,
Lovely days that used to be.

Now they've grown so strong and wise,
They don't need me when doubts arise.
But I need them to know they care,
I need old pleasures that made life fair.

Love, Sweet Pageant of a Lonely Life

Love, sweet pageant of a lonely life,
It came in all its glory for a little while,
A short sweet visit that had to end,
Leaving me alone, life's ways to wend!

In all its colors and in all its wealth,
Lovely beauty and flaming joy I felt.
Flaming joy and passion, and a sadness too,
That left tears in my eyes like drops of dew.

A sadness born of excruciating pain,
After a cloudless day, the heavy rain!
Oh! It was the usual, unrelenting end,
The joy and sadness that together blend!

Goodbye, my love, you gave me the greatest bliss,
Like the welcome rays of sun I felt your kiss.
But it had to end, and the aftermath is sad,
The interlude has left me pained but glad!

Glad to have known one like you,
To lift me out of the old aching blue.
Darling, my love, you've left but don't forget,
That one who loves you does love you yet!

The Heaving Waters of the Sea

The heaving waters of the sea
Bring memories back to me
The waves jump as if in plea
Hope surges, only fast to flee.

Currents dark, and whirlpools circling
Danger in its depths is lurking
Fearsome darkness, beauty besmirching
In my heart as I go on searching.

The waves are breaking, loudly calling
As they're spreading and they're sprawling
Murky waters over rocks are falling
Angry, threatening and mauling.

Take my heart and send it speeding
This bleeding heart needs love and healing
My spirit and my thoughts appealing
As on the banks I sit here kneeling.

Rough seas and surging waters keeling
Take from me all bitter feeling
Ease my pain and give me healing
Give my dead heart back its feeling.

Colleague

Colleague, colleague, my very dear,
I do hope you will not jeer.
But why do you leave me here,
Just because I sit so near?

I really do have such a fear,
As on the phone I look and peer,
While "boss" sits to the rear.
Lines are often not too clear,
And I can almost shed a tear,
As the red light does not appear.

With the receiver to my ear,
I try to catch names, I can't quite hear.
Oh, I sometimes feel so queer,
As surely all this does not cheer,
And does not help much to gear
Me to put on a bright veneer
And on the phone to sneer.

Oh, from the point I start to veer—
I should not my own name sear,
To hell with a damned career!

I Pray for You, My Darling

I pray for you, my darling
We'll be together again
Heartaches pass and love prevails
No need for sadness and wails.

We'll meet again my darling
When skies are blue and night is warm
True love does not know parting
And you shall hear me call.

I'll hear your voice so softly
And whispering your name
It will be called so loudly
In glory and in fame.

My voice will be so loving
You'll seek it out from all
You'll hear the thousand voices
But it's me you'll want to call.

For love reigns eternal
And wherever we may be
I'll see you in everything
Just as you will see me!

A little parting means just nought
In a little sadness we'll be caught
But then all will be well again
As in paradise love words we tell.

Dreamy Night

I've been so benumbed of late,
Drifting through deep starry skies,
A melancholy weighing so great,
The brightness in my eyes belies.

Some dreamy night I may forget
To return from a spangled dream,
And as a comet hurtles past,
I'll be part of its shining stream.

Soulmate

Soulmate, do you exist or not?
And if so, where are you and what?
Dreams are all that I have got.
Is only this cobwebby dream my lot?

My Sons

So handsome, so manly, so fine,
So proud I am of such as you.
All joys and happiness to you are due.
Dearer to me than life's very flame,
With you, I do not care for fame.

Sweet to me is to hear your name.
Dear ones, just keep on playing the game.
I wonder what the future will be
And think of what you mean to me.
For you're the glory, you're the ones
That I hold so close and say, "My sons."

Brave Bird

Its clipped, battered wings flapping helplessly
Against the roaring wind.
A tortured picture in valiant pain,
Against a backdrop of blue skies.

Like you, little bird,
I too gather strength and courage against all odds,
And, surrounded by the majesty of life,
I don't give up, but struggle bravely on.

My Blighted Flower

As I my lonely walk doth tread,
Memories sound their sad refrain,
Echoes of the past —
Drumming through my head,
Recall a love that was all in vain!

You were a gentle, blushing flower.
A flower that needed tender care,
I took you into my heart's bower,
And I kept you blooming there.

Alas, it was just for a while,
For I ceased to love your tender charms,
I became entranced with another's guile,
And she took your place within my arms.

I saw you wilt and fade away,
Your gentle spirit broken, crushed,
But a devil held me in its sway,
And all thoughts of you away I brushed.

Alack! at last there came the day
When we laid you down into the earth!
So angelic, in your white array,
And too late I realized your worth.

I had plucked you in your fullest bloom,
Then trampled o'er my treasured care.
But for my sin I live in gloom
Each hour I pay in full measure.

My tortured soul is racked in pain
How I miss you darling, God only knows
And I long for the hour we'll meet again
When your loving arms around me will close.

For I am sure you'll understand,
And forgiving, give me a chance anew,
We'll live together in the eternal land
Where mistakes are few and love is true.

A Happy Marriage is a Gift

A happy marriage is a gift
Enjoyed by few,
And this, my dear, I wish for you.
Caring, a love that's true,
Ever shining, ever new.
And through the years, more love accrue,
So may skies for you be ever blue.
But may you never be that hue.

Regrets

Sad I feel for all past years,
But my life's richer for bitter tears.
Time has sought deep pain to bring,
Crumbling my poor spirit's wing.

But I'm still able the sun to face,
And of my pain, I show no trace.
For when one has suffered enough,
The heart is built of firmer stuff.

A Prayer

I long to wander in the sky
While little fluffy clouds go by.
I'll dance around the moon up there
And find the answer to my prayer.
My song will echo through the sky
While falling stars go swiftly by.

Doggie

So human you look, so loving your eye.
For me, you will never die,
The sweetest soul with human eye.
I miss you, friend, but you're with me,
And this you'll be till eternity.
Our bond so deep, the love so great,
Though you left early and could not wait.
No goodbye did we share,
Not even a loving prayer.
I did not know that you'd be taken
To another world where you would waken.
My four-legged friend on golden sand,
In your heaven of Doggie-land,
Another path will walk again,
A path of joy—not knowing pain.

Relationships

In the name of love, maternal or paternal,
A soul is crushed, its confidence taken,
A heart is dead and will not awaken.

Love for man of woman, or woman of man,
Destroys a soul whose silent scream
No one hears—a nightmare dream!

Love, understanding, respect are fine,
Purifying, almost divine,
Uplifting, joyful, glorifying.

Its rare sweetness can be
A shining path to immortality,
Giving selfless joy—setting one free.

To My Boss

Dear V, you are the ideal boss.
We're devoted to you, you know.
If you leave, it will be a dead loss,
So we never want you to go.

V, for your good health we pray.
In sincerity, this we say
Whatever happens on life's way,
Your goodness and kindness sure will pay.

So you are an example to us
To be like you is a big plus,
A straight man with no fuss.
May all the world be made of such.

Love Unrequited

I say farewell,
No flowers, no words.
My pain I hide,
But you bright star I bring
An offering:
My love for you.

Much joy you gave,
A star that shines so bright,
Immortal beauty.
Without you,
What will I do?

My pain is mine, not yours.
My love is mine, not yours.
Still, I bring
My offering,
That precious thing:
My love for you.

Love, Sweet Pageant

Love, sweet pageant of a lonely life,
It came in all its glory for a little while.
A short sweet visit that had to end,
Leaving me alone life's ways to wend!

In all its colors and in all its wealth,
Lovely beauty and flaming joy I felt.
Flaming joy and passion and a sadness too,
That left the tears upon my eyes like drops of dew.

A sadness born of excruciating pain,
After a cloudless day the heavy rain!
Oh! it was the usual unrelenting end
The joy and sadness that together blend!!

Goodbye, my love, you gave me greatest bliss.
Like the welcome rays of sun, I felt your kiss.
But it had to end and the aftermath is sad,
The interlude has left me both pained and glad!

Glad to have known one like you
To lift me out of the old aching blue.
Darling, my love, you've left but don't forget,
That one who loves you does love you yet!!

Love

Tonight, I'll fly up to the moon.
My spirit will know no bars,
As your sweet melody will call
Me up beyond the stars.

Unity

We are both one world, one life,
And when we are apart,
My heart's as though pierced with a knife.
You are my very heart!

When things go wrong and I am sad,
And sleep is hard to find,
The thought of you brings peace
And gladness to my mind.

Eternal Shadows on the Wall

Shining moonlight on my bed,
Your form in glory on the wall.
But you are no more, as you are dead,
And in searing pain, your name I call.

Summertime

Summertime, summertime is the time for love,
Summertime when all is light and God's above.
Love, love, love, love that's in the air,
Here, there, and everywhere!

We feel so good, we laugh and sing,
We feel so full of health and zing.
Summertime is here to stay,
We hold our heads high and pray,

That summertime will always be
A time of hope for you and me,
A time to love, to trust, and hope,
Summertime brings so much scope.

Till We Meet Again

As on your way, my dear, you leave,
We must remember not to grieve.
But in a good future we must believe;
It's in your best interest that you know,
A future bright, with promise aglow.

So, we must part with joy, we know!
Be on your way, and God bless.
You've earned good days, with no more stress,
So we wish you joy and all success!

Eye of the Storm

Little glistening diamond,
Shining, glittering drop of dew,
Bitter symbol of pain and fear,
Decades of silent misery.
"Why! Oh why!" I ask,
As I gaze upon this sparkling tear.

Scapegoat to a psychotic mind,
Tortured, crucified till the end!
Yet you refuse to make amends.
The years of sorrow have taken their toll.
Freed, I go to eternal rest,
But you—the Devil has your soul.

Song of a Pensioner

I wake every morning, come rain or shine,
To know that this day is mine.
To move into that mad rush hour,
Trapped in traffic or a heavy shower.

I've worked all my life and taken a battering,
The noise of office work bugging and shattering.
The ring of telephones so loud and shrill,
Never a moment to be quiet or still.

Now I have time to see clouds on high,
Moving peacefully across a bright azure sky.
Each morning, I wake to the song of birds,
The evening brings calm and peace beyond words.

Be Merry

Let's drink, be merry, and gay,
It's a lovely, lovely day.
Many anniversaries to come,
Many parties with songs to hum.

Raise our glasses in good cheer,
And do the same for many a year.
Our friends so good, so very dear,
In our hearts are always near.

Peach

With grand passion, I feast upon your flawless beauty,
Eyes glazed in anticipation of your divine touch.
Upon my lips, your exotic, glowing perfection
Stirs the beast in me, as I
Voraciously relish the pinkish flush
Upon the golden satin skin.
My passion soars to heavenly bliss.
Reaching out to clasp you tenderly,
Raising your loveliness to my lips,
Perfection disappears in noisy, greedy sips.
Oh! The sad fate of this ripe, luscious peach!

To Albert

Albert, dear son, we love you so,
Loving you, we want you to know.
Be wherever you are, our blessings will go,
Ever our love for you will flow.
Remember that we love you, though
Time made you from a babe to grow.

To a fine young man who will show
All that you can, set the world aglow.
Lambkin you were not so long ago,
Knowing you as a child, now a man you grow.
Extend our love and good wishes to you,
Remember, true son of ours, we LOVE YOU SO.

To My Workmate

Lady, you are so very nice,
Full of wit, sparkle, and spice.
A "toughie," but we love you so,
That I'm sure you already know.
Lady, you are my friend,
And I hope you'll be till life's end.

No Pledge

The last time you left, I ran away too,
To join my good friends so loyal and true:
The harsh winds, grey clouds, and foaming sea.
But I am not happy; I wish I were free.

Begging for forgiveness, you ask for a kiss
To pledge the future of unsheltered bliss.
But what you don't know is that I have won
A silver cup in my race to the sun,

A cup so full of silver stars,
With golden chips from the far planet Mars,
Sapphire stars from skies so blue.
No, I can't fill my cup with a pledge to you.

Traffic

Twinkling, blinking fireflies,
Rows of flashing lights gliding in the gloom,
Thousands of weekend revelers returning,
Bulky metal wheels rotating.

Shadows in the darkening gloom,
Each a lethal weapon of doom!
The ever-growing traffic of this century—
Where will it end?
When will it end?

Soon from the air shall we descend!
Technology's revenge:
Pollution,
Congestion,
Confusion,
Daily nerves and irritation,
A hefty price for sophistication.

Comfort

When it's time for sleeping
But sleep is hard to woo,
I close my eyes and think of love,
And love is you!

And if things go contrarywise
And sleep is hard to find,
The thought of you brings
Peace and gladness to my mind.

And though the sun somehow seems
Not so bright when we're apart,
The thought of you brings
Light and sunshine to my heart.

Passing Years

I think as I mope in my house each day,
How I'm now lonely, frail, and grey.
The children have grown, as it must be;
They no longer have much need of me.

I dream of all the years gone by
When I knew to answer their call or cry,
Sons and daughters sat on my knee—
Lovely days that used to be.

Now they've grown so strong and wise,
They don't need me when doubts arise.
But I need them, to know they care;
I need old pleasures that made life fair.

My Grandson

I pick up the phone for a moment of bliss,
I talk to my love and send him a kiss.
"How are you?" I ask, and he says
His sister is "very poorly",
Then, "Bye now," he says, "the boss is here!"
Oh, his language is so very unclear!

Well, this child of the nineties lives not near,
The thoughts don't exactly cheer,
But my darling grandson is from Yorkshire.

The Days Are Long

The days are long,
The nights are sad,
The hours and minutes drag.
Oh, love of my life, I miss you so,
But this you do not even know.

Oh, my dear, how will it end?
Will my broken heart ever mend?
I live with hurt and with despair;
Joy to me is a thing so rare!

Oh, dearest love, come back to me,
We'll start again the rhapsody.
Oh, my love, please hear my cry,
For if you don't, I shall surely die!

Love

My love for you goes deep and true,
I can't believe that I love you.
The feeling is yet so new,
Morning glory, fresh drops of dew.

Of love, I've known just a few,
But none of this caliber and hue.
I feel like a caged bear in a zoo,
Repressed, waiting for you to woo,
Wondering whether you love me too,
Waiting, waiting for just a cue!

Or just a sign from you,
Over the months my love just grew.
I long for you, I long for you,
Sweetheart of mine, I so love you!

Life

Sad I feel for all past years,
But my life's richer for bitter tears.
Time has sought deep pain to bring,
Crumbling my poor spirit's wing.

But I'm still able the sun to face,
And of my past, I show no trace.
For when one has suffered enough,
The heart is built of stronger stuff.

Good Luck

Going are you both so far away,
Oh! When we'll meet, we cannot say.
Once again, we'll meet together one day,
Dear ones, good fortune light your way!

Long ways together will go you two,
Under far skies a life anew!
Come the day we'll again meet you,
Keepsake small — fondness true!

And may skies for you be ever blue!

Parting is Sad

Parting is sad, and we feel bad,
Though for you, we should be glad.
We'll miss you, friend, very much,
But wish you luck and other such.

Happy times for all of you,
Our wishes from us are so true.
May every joy be yours, with love,
And blessings from the Lord above.

Till we meet again, then, all the best,
We'll think of you, though you go west!
Good luck, meantime, six months will pass,
Your family will grow and joy amass.

Till we meet again.

To Mella

Mella dear, you have always been,
A dear good friend to me.
Though this I've not always seen,
I admit, in all humility.

But now I do so realize,
And appreciate wholeheartedly,
How kind you are, and good and wise,
How dear you are to me.

I'm truly sad we won't now be,
Because of circumstances, unfortunately,
So much in each other's company,
But we'll always keep contact, to that I'll see.

Till 120, as they say,
May roses and happiness bless your way,
For this I wish and pray.
And good friends we shall always stay.

I wish you "till 120" as they say,
May roses and happiness shower your way,
For this I deeply hope and pray,
Good friends we shall always stay.

Whispered Words

I recall the whispered words
That you left behind,
As the sweetest scented evening brings you back to mind.
Rapturous love, for me the very first,
And of that love, I still feel a thirst.

My life won't even hold a cup of wine so clear;
The poignant thought fills my mind with fear.
Eternally enthralling, youth, so full of glorious dreaming,
Forever sparkling, shining, gleaming.

I thought we would never meet again,
Worlds apart, living through our pain.
But as our lonely lives we wind and wend,
We know we'll meet again at journey's end.

For love like ours knows neither bolts nor bars,
And we shall meet again beyond the stars.

Friends

Dearest, kind friends I have, to soothe and love,
Your gentle arms enfolding me ever.
You're like pure shining angels from above,
Such friendship even death will not sever.

Sweet angels of compassion and good cheer,
Tending me with such care and devotion.
Ever with me, my friends who are so dear,
Your friendship moves me to deep emotion.

Such pure friendship is so holy and sweet,
And as night approaches, I have no fear.
Deep gratitude I feel with each heartbeat,
Because I know that you are ever near.

Darkness approaches and life ebbs and wanes,
Yet my heart's light—my life's not been in vain.

Mother

Dear mother, you are now so far away,
But my need for you is still so very great.
You are not here to guide and show the way,
But you have taught me how to fight my fate.

Patience and fortitude were unknown to me,
But those you tried to impart to me.
Harsh and hot-headed I was prone to be,
But you taught me courage, serenity, and sympathy.

Though many long miles there are between us today,
I still can prove that I'm your daughter true.
I'll follow the right path and will not stray,
That's the very least that I can do for you.

I'll take your example and be wise and good,
And be a good and virtuous person as you are.
And like you, be a good mother to my brood;
I shall be paying in some measure for your tender care.

That's the very least I can now do for you,
A credit to a good mother be.

Grandchild

My friend, now you are blessed
With a grandchild to give you joy.
May she grow with love and zest,
Happiness with every quest.

May you have many grandchildren more,
Coming and going through your door,
Making children's usual uproar.
Voices merrily will soar,
Faces turned to you, so pure.

We know that for you it's sure
That your first grandchild is born.
May many such blessings your life adorn.
Good luck on this happy event;
We know how much this has meant.

The hours of expectation spent,
On your trip to Italy as you went.
May your grandchild grow to be strong and fine,
Bringing joy one can't define.
May God's blessings on her shine.

My friend, may you and your wife be blessed
With many, many grandchildren to attest.
Future fruitful years of jest,
And laughter, fun, and all the best.

May your years be filled with bliss;
We wish you every happiness.
To your grandchild, we give a kiss
As life's blessings on the child we wish.

Mother
(1958)

In my heart, there is a sharp need,
I think of you with breaking heart and cry.

Oh, for the balm to stop my heart to bleed,
I can only think of you with love, and sigh!

You were with me through all the growing years,
In all my troubles, you were there to guide.

You gave me strength and allayed my fears,
From you, I had no nagging fear to hide.

Dear Mother

Mother, how I realize your worth,
Oh! dearest person on all the earth.
There was around you joy and mirth,
How you always managed to hide your pain and hurt.
Ever loving, though I was often curt,
Reasonable and sweet, there's goodness in your heart.

New York, New York

Crowded roads, dangerous and pulsating,
Thronging flesh, a mechanical gyrating.
Tall buildings proudly silhouetted against the skyline,
Stupendous, fascinating and exciting.
Wildly exhilarating, heartbreaking, and stimulating,
Uniquely cosmopolitan, crossroads of life.
RED
BIG APPLE,
New
York.

Love's Illusion

Idyllic beauty turned to dust,
Love's illusion, gold turned to rust.
End of a rainbow, end of dreams,
Shattered into smithereens.

A Eulogy — for My Brother

Our brother, friend, role model,
You made the world a richer place,
And will continue to give light to all
Wherever you are today.

You were an inspiration loved by all;
Hundreds came to bid farewell,
Ministers, mayors, religious, secular,
Muslims, Christians, Arabs, Druze.
The abundance of wreaths and flowers
spoke of the many who loved you.

Whoever knew you was enriched by your magical warmth,
Love, compassion.
We feel so lost without you but will carry on,
Tears in our hearts, smiles on our faces.
Though gone on your spiritual quest,
Our hearts will always hold you.

Shining Lights

In the still of the night,
I see a light,
Shining, calling,

Oh, so bright!
I fear for you and hold you tight
In the deep, dark still of the night.

Life's Joyous Gifts

Trees abloom and flowers bright,
Blue skies, deep seas, a world of delight.
Rocky hills, winding streams,
Beauty to behold,
A sunset ablaze with red and gold.

Soft clouds rushing in pursuit,
Birds warbling on ripe, luscious fruit,
A bouncing baby on mother's knee,
Life's charms are for all to see.

A pretty garden the dew caresses,
These are treasures Man possesses.
To God's great gifts we must relate,
For then we will have no grudge with fate.

To My Beloved Lishai

My beautiful princess, I love you so;
This you must always know.
And if ever you're sad and feeling blue,
Think of my great love for you.

Unemployment

She doesn't yell or scream aloud,
Her head held high, as yet unbowed.
Her heart is full of pain and tears,
The sadness of all passing years.

She's waiting, hoping for the day
When her many troubles will go away.
She raises her head towards the sky
And lets out a silent, poignant cry.

No home, no money coming in,
No chance a new life to begin.
Fighting hard not to go under,
Yet her very soul is torn asunder.

Hush, my dear, the dawn will come,
Keep hope and see the rising sun.
The rainbow comes out after rain,
And joy will enter your heart again.

A Prayer

I long to wander in the sky
While little fluffy clouds go by.
I'll dance through all the steps up there
And find the answer to my prayer.

My song will echo through the sky
While falling stars go swiftly by.

Happiness

Years from the present time,
I may just find
A different way to wend,
A greener hill to climb.

Maybe a velvety plain
Will spread before my steps,
And I'll behold its beauty and know it's mine.

Until that fateful day,
Till that glorious hour does fall,
I must find another way
And follow a different call.

Now I must be content to stay,
To watch the sun dip low,
And seeing its glory, pray
That joy and love I'll know.

To a Friend

I'm lucky to have you as a friend,
For a true friend is a real godsend.
She gives concern and care without end,
And pain and sorrow she helps to mend.

True friends are like angels of light,
With a powerful, godly force and might,
Leading one through the darkness of night,
Guiding and helping to do what's right.

Your friendship means so much to me,
For through the darkness, I can see
The beauty that in life can be
Enhanced by someone such as thee.

To Brother Jackie
on His Birthday

A torch in darkness, giving light,
To know you is joy and delight.
Your ready smile and face so bright,
A shining moon in the midst of night.

With a helping hand in others' plight,
You always seem to make things right.
A family must in love unite.

Refuge

Mid starry skies, there lies a land
With lovely flowers and glowing sand,
A land of hope and trust and love,
A land of light and joy above.

At ninety, how much more is there?
I wonder when, I wonder where.
I'll be in that glorious atmosphere,
Its bright rays of light are drawing near.

Shimmering pastels tinged with gold,
Drawing near and taking hold
Of this body so worn and weary,
Of this life that's now so dreary.

The aches and pains will all be gone,
And a new body I will don.
I'll soar up to the sparkling moon,
And death will be a godly boon.

Goodbye

(Written when I was 16 years old)

Life is fading fast,
Shadows of the past,
Voices sobbing low,
While away I go.

Sweeter than the spring,
Lovelier than day,
Gentle as a dove
Is my lady love.

Dearer than my life
Is my darling wife.
True love from her springs
On eternal wings.

Angel by my side,
While away I ride,
Her hands clasped in prayer,
Left in God's good care.

One day we shall meet,
I'll be there to greet
My mate when she comes
To God's garden above.

Then goodbye, my sweet,
Till again we meet.
Darling, you'll come there,
Answering my prayer.

To another world I go,
Leaving you in woe.
But before I leave,
I ask you not to grieve.

Farewell, farewell, my dearest heart,
The time has come for us to part.
Goodbye, my wife, so good and wise,
We'll meet again in paradise.

To Jack

Dear Jack, you've made your mark in life,
It's a joy to know you and Babs, your wife.
We're lucky to have you as a friend,
For a true friend is a godsend.

True friends are like angels of light,
With a powerful, godly force and might.
Your friendship means so much to me,
For through the darkness, I can see
The beauty that in life can be
Enhanced by someone such as thee.

Encased

I am a pearl
Embedded in an oyster.
No thought, no feeling,
No flight,
No respite.

Expression?
Not for me.
Lost in the world,
Breathing but not living,
Lost in the darkness of gloom,
Locked in impending doom—
A lost pearl.

Departed

He gave up nothing, though he left his all,
Reluctantly answered the mystic call.
Offerings of sweet-scented flowers
Will keep him company with the stars.

But when dark night its course has run,
He'll fly, soaring to the morning sun.
He has a pilgrimage to make,
To be at one with all eternity.
But though he never now will wake,
Part of him lives on with me.

He left us with wings unfurled
And now belongs to another world.
Woven, shiny dreams lost on the way,
Shattered fragments here to stay.

Farewell, your sorrows are now past;
Your anguished soul finds peace at last.
Your troubled heart has found its rest,
As an angel takes you to its breast.

Departed Friend

For another friend I'm left to grieve,
Our days of friendship we can't retrieve.
Except in memories of past pleasure,
Times have passed in joy and leisure.

Dearest friend, time ran out so fast,
As I think of days now past,
My heart breaks to think we'll meet no more,
Except perhaps on some distant shore.

I hope and pray that this shall be,
That once again your face I'll see,
That we shall happily meet again,
Where skies are blue and there's no pain.

So, I'll wait patiently for that day
When I shall also come away.
I'll see dear faces on the other side,
As into a tunnel of light my soul will glide.

The Gleam of Firelight

In the gleam of firelight, your dear face I see,
Darkness falls; the long night lies before me.
I turn and toss and will myself to sleep,
My hot tears fall as I try not to weep.

Trees swinging in the night breeze,
Shadows falling on the earth, and on the wall they tease.
Heart heavy, I fight the weight,
Heartbeats come at such a fast rate.

Melancholy

Falling like a heavy sheet,
A cloak of black from head to feet.
The morning sun sheds golden rays,
The sky with diamonds and pearly days.

Each day I pass after another sleepless night,
Another day to raise my head and fight.

Stardust

I have been so benumbed of late,
Drifting through deep starry skies,
A melancholy weighing so great
The brightness in my eyes belies.

Some dreary night I may float,
To return from a spangled dream,
And as a comet hurtles past,
I'll be part of its shining stream.

A Prayer

I wish to wander in the sky
While little fluffy clouds pass by.
I'll dance through all the stars up there
And find the answers to my prayer.

My prayer will echo through the sky
While falling stars go swiftly by.

Absence

When you have left to go so far,
In my sad heart it seems
My life is empty of happiness,
So devoid of dreams.

When evening shadows dance and play,
My heart feels the dark night.
But I reach and search in vain
For a starry light.

When you have left and gone so far,
My heart does only know
My steps must quickly follow you
Wherever you go.

Friends

My dear good friend, always there
When I am sad and alone,
She takes my anguish away,
And makes the pain her own.

Her friendship does not fade away
When darkness falls and strong winds blow,
But like the warmth of happiness and joy,
She cheers me when I'm feeling low.

She's such a faithful, loving friend
That whatever my lot may be,
She's my rainbow in the stormy strife,
And my anchor in the sea of life.

Escape

Part of me lingered,
Captive with you,
Till I found you again
Midst glistening dew.

Caught by your finger,
Trapped in a shell,
Now you don't know me,
Whom you knew so well.

I've escaped far away
In a languishing swoon,
Hurtling through starlight
To the beckoning moon.

Old Pleasures

I think as I mope in my house each day,
How I am lonely, old, and gray.
The children have grown, as it must be;
They no longer have much need of me.

I dream of all the years gone by
When I used to answer their call or cry.
Sons and daughters sat on my knee—
Lovely days that used to be.

Now they've grown so strong and wise,
They don't need me when troubles arise.
But I need them, to know they care;
I need old pleasures that made life fair.

Dear Mother, Far Away

Dear mother, you are now so far away,
But my need for you is still so very great.
You are not here to guide and show the way,
But you have taught me how to fight my fate.

Patience and fortitude were unknown to me,
But these two virtues you tried to impart to me.
Hasty and hot-headed I was prone to be,
But you taught me courage, serenity, and sympathy.

Though many long miles are between us today,
I still can prove that I'm your child so true.
I'll follow the right path and will not stray,
That's the very least that I can do for you.

And if I take your example and be wise and good,
And be a good and virtuous woman as you say,
And like you, be a good mother to my brood,
I shall be paying in some measure for your tender care.

That's the very least I can now do for you—
A credit to a good mother be.

Lost Love

Sitting by the window, hearing the rain
So softly patter on the windowpane,
My thoughts guide me back down memory lane
To a dear lost love I'll never meet again.

I cry your name in deep despair,
In poignant pain, so hard to bear.
Love such as ours, so fine, so rare,
Was, after all, a doomed affair.

Longing, dreaming, crying, yearning,
My very soul is searing, burning.
With joy and pain, my heart is churning,
Glimpses of heaven and hell discerning.

The rain has stopped; there's a deep calm,
Enveloping me like a healing balm.
Though imprisoned in a wall of time,
Love remains glorious and sublime.

Infallible

Metallic bird flying way up high,
Massive monster of the sky.
Through the golden mantle of sunlight,
A velvet cloak of darkest night.

Through heavy sleet or slashing rain,
This brave product of the human brain.
But not infallible,
Hurtling through space and air,
To death, destruction, and despair.
No, not infallible.

The Child and Man

When I look at a child's sweet, shining face,
A child's beguiling smile,
The innocence, trust, and winning ways,
I cannot but pause awhile

And wonder how these children can grow
Into grumpy and frowning old folk,
Distrusting, complaining, and full of woe.
Oh, life's a cruel joke.

Homeless

Clothed in tattered rags,
Belongings packed in paper bags.
Nowhere to go—no food to eat,
His life and breath are on the street.

A broken life gone awry,
No shelter from a blazing sky.
Life's sorrows have taken a toll
Upon his body and his soul.

His brain is cracked as his broken dream,
His heart is full of a silent scream.
The pain that life has thought to bring
Has crumpled up his spirit's wing.

No tender care, no sweet caress
To give redemption from the mess.
No one to grieve or understand
When death extends its bony hand.

There but for the grace of God go I,
And yet I do not even try
To alleviate his wretched state,
As I leave him to his awful fate.

Invitation to Love

I'm the solid, stable earth,
You're the leaf upon the tree.
Come a day you'll float to me,
Drifting softly, falling free.

You're a raindrop, I'm the sea.
Come a day you'll flow to me,
Downward falling, softly calling.
I'm the ocean, come to me.

Come to love, come to live.
Come and share it, take and give.
Come to love, come and be
Mine forever, come to me!

Regret

Sad I feel for all past years,
But my life's richer for bitter tears.

Time has sought deep pain to bring,
Crumbling my poor spirit's wing.

But I'm still able the sun to face,
And of my pain, I show no trace.

For when one has suffered enough,
The heart is built of firmer stuff.

Brave Bird

Its clipped and battered wings
Flapping helplessly against the beating wind.

A tortured picture of valiant pain
Against a backdrop of blue skies.

Like you, little bird, I too gather
Strength and courage against all odds.

And, surrounded by the majesty of life, I don't give up,
But, albeit haltingly,
Struggle bravely on!

Adieu

He gave up nothing, though he left his all,
Reluctantly answered the mystic call.
Offerings of sweet-scented flowers
Will keep him company with the stars.
But when dark night its course has run,
He'll fly, soaring to the morning sun.

He has a pilgrimage to make,
Though now he will never wake.
Yet he'll be at one with eternity,
While part of him lives on in me.

He left us with wings unfurled
And now belongs to another world.
Woven dreams lost on the way,
Shattered fragments here to stay.

Farewell, your sorrows are now past;
Your anguished soul finds peace at last.
Your troubled heart has found its rest,
As an angel takes you to its breast.

Refusal

The last time you left, I ran away too
To join good friends so loyal and true:
The harsh winds, grey clouds, and foaming sea.
But I'm not happy; I wish I were free.

Begging forgiveness, you ask for a kiss,
A pledge to a future of unshattered bliss.
But what you don't know is that I have won
A silver cup in my race to the sun.

A cup so full of shining stars,
With golden chips from planet Mars,
Sapphire studs from skies so blue.
No, I can't fill my cup with a pledge to you.

Farewell
(Love Unrequited)

I say farewell,
No flowers, no words—
My pain I hide,
But you bright star I bring
An offering—
My love for you.

Much joy you gave,
Bright star that shines so strong,
Immortal beauty.
Without you,
What will I do?

My pain is mine, not yours,
My love is mine, not yours.
Still, I bring
My offering,
Dear precious thing—
My love for you!

Sunrise — Sunset

My ship glides proudly by on glistening waves,
Beneath a canopy of blue skies,
Bright sunshine flashing through its wide portholes.

Soon the sun will set in all its glory,
My ship, a dark shadow of its former self,
Will sail on rougher waters to oblivion.

Jeremy Michael Samuel

Jeremy is so jolly a boy
Ever laughing, he's his parents' joy
Running about the house as he plays
Ever endearing are all his ways.
May his life be good and actions kind,
Years of gladness may his footsteps wind.

Mama and Papa, he's learnt to say,
It turns their hearts, brings light to their day
Calling him "Michael" his second name
Has become a habit, being more plain
Anyhow he answers to either name
Everything for him is one big joke
Life for him does not provoke.

So dear child the years will come and go
And you may sorrow and trouble not know
May you then be bright as you are now
Under no events furrow your brow
Ever showing a spirit true
Living as your parents wish you to.

Self-Annihilation

Billowing silvery waves draw near
Fill my head with abounding fear
My motive is as yet unclear
As rolling waves temptingly appear.

Twin contrary voices I seem to hear
One despairing, "End it — come on — don't veer."
The wiser voice, calming and clear
"Beware - your good name don't smear."

"Don't you, can't you, won't you see?
To master pain is victory.
The body's pain you can placate
But your soul's rights you'll confiscate."

"Take courage and just keep on
Till earthly days naturally have gone."
So — thank God, this battle I have won
And for me a new life has begun.

Golden Fruit

With grand passion,
I feed upon your flawless beauty.
My eyes glazed with anticipation
of your divine touch on my lips.

Your beautiful, glowing, exotic perfection
brings out the beast in me
as I note your delicate flush.

Pinkish blush upon the golden shine.
My passion soars to a climax
as I reach out my hand
and clasp you tenderly,
raising your beauty to my lips.

Perfection disappears in quiet greed.
The fate of this ripe, perfect peach.

A Tear — Symbol of Sorrow

Little glistening diamond
Shining, glittering drop of dew
Bitter symbol of pain and fear
Decades of silent misery
Why, oh why, I ask
Looking upon this sparkling tear.

Scapegoat to a psychotic mind
Their years they took their toll
Tortured, crucified till the end!
Yet you refuse to make amend.

The years of sorrow have taken toll
Freed, I go to eternal rest
But you — the Devil has your soul.

Perfection
(Barbie Doll)

Long legs, small waist,
Perfect body
Oh so slim
Exquisite beauty
Firm & trim
So flexible!
So irresistible!

I envy you! You have it all.
My lovely little Barbie doll.

A Rose so Fair

Red is the rose that unfolds at dawn
Its beauty so fresh with bloom
Sweet is the face that shines at morn
She does not realize her doom.

Lovely, the rose with fragrance sweet
As its petals open and spread.
Fair is her face and proud her feet
For tomorrow she is to wed.

The white noon of the sun shines bright
Ah, Rose! your petals droop and fade.
The girl turned to woman — unable to fight
Victim of selfish Man's need she's made.

The sunset shines in gold and flame
The lovely rose is dying away...
It has lived its day and played the game
And now it does not want to stay.

The lady with the white hair strands
Her sunset also now draws near
She waits her doom with folded hands
Her brow serene and without fear

The years have passed, the children grown
So many more have come to stay
Her work perhaps may remain unknown
Does it matter if she goes away?

So, life goes on and on and on
Its currents swiftly passing by
But woman's place is like the rose
To bloom, to suffer, and to cry!

Bye for Now

When you have left to go so far
In my heart it seems
My life is empty of happiness
So devoid of dreams.

When evening shadows dance and play
My heart feels the dark night
And I search and search in vain
For a starry light.

When you have gone so far
My heart does only know
My steps must quickly follow you
Wherever you may go.

www.ingramcontent.com/pod-product-compliance
Lightning Source LLC
Chambersburg PA
CBHW031434120626
46545CB00006B/2404